GW00457984

Always happiest on a beach.
Running and music are my inner freedom and peace.
To my adult kids, what a journey, I adore you.

Freda – Always there and my biggest supporter.

Theresa – Who Always wants to believe.

Radha – My biggest cheerleader.

My Sissy – Thank you for your time.

"Women's true soulmates are our girlfriends."

Clara Dakota

MIDLIFE CRISIS

AUSTIN MACAULEY PUBLISHERS™

LONDON • CAMBRIDGE • NEW YORK • SHARJAH

A CIP catalogue record for this title is available from the British Library.

ISBN 9781398422285 (Paperback)
ISBN 9781398422292 (Hardback)
ISBN 9781398422308 (ePub e-book)

www.austinmacauley.com

First Published 2022
Austin Macauley Publishers Ltd®
1 Canada Square
Canary Wharf
London
E14 5AA

So, after 20 years in the UK/US and 20+ years of marriage, there was an awakening.

My husband and I had hit an impasse.

I am originally from the UK and my husband is from the US. We met in the UK on a blind date and the rest is, as they say, history.

When we met, he was cool, calm and mirrored my personality so well that he was just a Male version of me, looking back on that now, I should have seen some red flags, I was so happy that I had found someone that engaged me, he listened and loved my sense of humour, he loved my boys and loved to play as he was a big funny child himself, what fun we all used to have! We used to put a pin in a map at the weekends and just go, wherever we ended up was always filled with laughter and light heartedness, and the sex…so great and connected on a level I'd never felt before.

After a few years of not so high-level jobs and some degrees and certifications he became happily engrossed in becoming a 'Workaholic' and I had become happily engaged in raising my kids and having a better life, within the relationship and of course financially too. Dealing with the cycle of moving every three years to continue in the search for his 'Perfect role' or the 'Pay that he deserved' was difficult, but I felt like I had to support him.

Moving seemed to be in our blood, but looking back now, I think I just went with the flow to much just so he could follow his dreams! I also see that I was too pliable and should have spoken up, but I was feeling the change in me even then.

We lived in the UK in numerous places and then the 9/11 terror attacks happened in the US, the kids were still young back then and he was feeling the pull of his Family back to the US, we talked at great length about the pros and cons of moving to the US and ultimately, we decided to move to the US looking for his new 'Perfect job' and also to be closer to his family. We moved in with his Parents initially and I built and amazing relationship with them and that will always be a blessing for me, they were both wonderful people who I dearly loved. After a few years of re-establishing ourselves, and a couple of job moves from MN to SD he did get a good job with great pay with a golden ball and chain pension scheme. He seemed like this job completed him and the monetary gain made him as happy as I had ever seen him but with that money came a disconnect that would signal the beginning of a whole new version of him.

Meanwhile, our youngest daughter was struggling with some health issues which later turned out to be Crohn's disease, so another thing to add to the busy list of parenting duties to keep me from not seeing the wood for the trees!

I recall a particular difficult transition to a place where my husband had already moved before the rest of the family, and I might add, bought a house I had only seen online!

My middle son was a senior in High School that year, and now looking back, it was the worst move for our family.

There was a day not so long during my son's first term that he texted me in the morning, and wrote, "I am sitting in the toilet cubicle at school, will you come get me so we can have lunch together?" and to say it broke my heart will be the biggest understatement.

Something in me changed that day, yet I was unaware of what that was and to what depths…

My lost son finally met a girl in High School who befriended him and all was finally good in his world. Young love was all healing but the Family dynamic had changed for sure.

At my job in this town, I was confronted with a strange situation. There was a lovely, lost and homeless pregnant girl who ended up living with us for a while. She stayed till after her baby was born, and being at the birth was a gift I shall never forget. Looking back to that time my kids were invested in this experience, but not him. He was alright to spend the money she needed but he never engaged her. Looking back, it was just another 'wood for the trees' situation, but I was still oblivious! Sadly, this lost young girl was killed in a car accident four years later; I am so glad that my children and I were part of her and her daughter's life.

My husband got another big raise and another big bonus, he thought he had achieved the career pinnacle and everything he had ever been searching for, or so he thought…

During this time there were lots of expensive trips, shopping, new cars and gifts, but a separation for him and I on a whole new level. His job, although was everything he had ever wanted, was slowing but surely killing his spirit. A lot of morally questionable things were happening in the workplace and the money kept on rolling in to keep the executive team in its place and quiet.

Slowly, he was realising he was not able to continue at such a pace and the morally bankrupt behaviour of that Company was killing him inside. The pay raises/bonuses would placate his fears for six months of the year then he would spiral for the remaining six months. I wondered what the catalyst would be!

During the space of the next three years, my grandmother passed away. Then his father died after a short illness, then my mom died and then his mom died! I think that was what began the unravelling...

Slowly but surely I saw a shift in him. He closed himself off emotionally (and physically) to me and the children. He was not sleeping at night but took his naps to a whole new level. He did not process nor grieve any of the aforementioned deaths, and I knew trouble was brewing.

During a surreal trip to New Orleans where too much alcohol and lots of private dancers in back rooms were enmeshed into a 'perfect storm'. That weekend changed the way I thought about him forever. On the way back home, we talked about our weekend and he refused to admit that the happenings of the previous night were anything but drunken malarkey. That behaviour was not the man I used to know but the musings of a broken man looking for an out. An out from me or us or himself, I was not sure at this point. It was however the game changer for me, but I was not sure how to proceed.

Not long after that night, he and his toxic work parted ways after they mutually agreed that he could never 'fit in' there. He would not bend to their will anymore. During this time there was no talking, no discussion of what was next and a complete disconnect for him and I.

He took on another job in the interim, and this was all decided without consulting me. He decided to live out of the state Monday through Friday and return at the weekends. The emotional disconnect was pronounced and parading around our house like the strippers he refused to admit he entertained!

After we lived separately during the week for a little while, the emotional and physical disconnect was complete. After a particularly bad bout of the man-flu and his decision to live above a nightclub he realised that his choices were not really working for him, he then suggested that we should consider going back to the UK to try to make our relationship work, and he agreed he needed to slow down the pace of his work life. Deep down I knew that we were struggling to connect on any level, and I had been asking for change for a couple of years now, but to no avail. I felt like I had to take a stand and to be honest before we moved back to the UK. I informed him that I will not ask for change anymore, that he can just continue on pleasing himself and I shall now start doing the same. He seemed shocked by this revelation when our cycle consisted of, me telling him how good it used to be and how I missed that and him. Then that was met with 7-10 days of reconnection then the imminent disconnect. It was always heart-breaking to watch him separate from me again and just getting on with his own life with no regard for us. Part of me thinks he just needs a companion that will be available for the hour or so that he needs to talk per day, he can moan and complain then he just wants to go off and do his own thing, which meets none of my needs. although that is exactly what he had been doing these lasty few years!

So off we went again, next stop: the UK.

He spent 13 months looking for a job here as apparently it is really hard to get a job without having a job. During this period, he was as isolated as I had ever seen him. Drinking too much, sleeping all day and up all night. He was disconnected from his few friends in the US and I was no longer keeping communication open with them or his family in the US, so loneliness consumed him.

Finally, after 13 months he did get a job taking half the pay that he received in the US, but he was happy that someone wanted him. Now, he is at another job which he is not happy in, where he doesn't feel he is worthy, appreciated, nor compensated enough and his job is still apparently the most important job in the world! Sensing my sarcasm?

During his narcissistic rants about him, him and more him, he continually muses that he feels like he is never compensated enough or able to make the changes he wants within any work environment. My feeling is that no job will ever satisfy because he himself is unhappy.

We are currently doing counselling with an amazing Lady who totally gets our dynamic. I have discovered that I can be closed off and sometimes cold to protect myself and although being self-aware is important; counselling makes my 'stiff upper lip', cringe a little bit. His lightbulb moments were that he is the 'I am never good enough' and 'I do not want to stand out' guy. He just wants to fade into the background in the real world but he also wants to shine within a work environment, and all of that is difficult when you are seven feet tall! I was unaware how all the height shaming, pointing, staring and comments had affected him and his personality since childhood. Also, the Golden Child syndrome has affected his life too. During this time, he started to do lots of "Work trips" and spending every moment not spent working or napping on his devices. The red flags were certainly mounting but there I was, still feeling bad for him and wishing for the old version of us to reappear.

I am now on the other side of Menopause, although that had its own challenges, I do love how there is zero room for procrastinating, BS or anything that does not align with my life's purpose. I have embraced that change and am always confused when people say that they wish they could go back in time. I have never felt more 'put together' mentally than I do right now, yet my world is imploding but I understand it is necessary.

I recently started working in a local upscale office. I have to be honest and say that getting out of the daily drama of him and his impending doom and mood swings was liberating. After a few weeks of socialising with the locals and befriending my work colleagues, I did feel an impending doom at the prospect of going home at the end of the day, so I pondered if this was the time for the end to begin. After a particularly busy weekend something literally flipped in me. It was hard to hold back the tears that day, but I just knew I had to say it and so I drove home, crying all the way I might add.

I opened the front door and went and sat in the living room, still crying I sat and waited for him to look at me and actually 'see me'. He was on his computer, cursing about something he was doing and did not see me. He then went upstairs, walking past me whilst I was still crying and he did not even look in my direction, for about an hour he was gone, and so I calmed myself. When he returned, I was no longer crying but strong and determined. This just proved to me that this was over for me and for him too.

When he returned, I felt sick and was shaking but said, "I do not think I can do this anymore," to which his reply was "I am so glad you brought this up as I was trying to find the words too." My bitchy cold side wanted to retort with, "and how long would you let this go on for," but I resisted that urge.

So after saying the words 'I cannot do this anymore' a strange and surreal 24 hours ensued where I felt as sexually attracted to him as I had ever felt. We talked, went to the movies, "Once Upon a Time in Hollywood" of all movies. He ate nachos and we talked about what we would do in our new lives. We laughed about how he could never be alone as he is not built that way; and we talked about going to Spain for a week over Christmas!

I asked him if we could have sex but he turned me down saying it would be "too hard for him emotionally." After the "No" I felt a wave of such deep grief that I started crying and could not stop. It was hard to breathe, yet all I wanted to do was to scream and hold him so tight. He did comfort me, but at a distance if that makes sense. I leaned into him and held his arm so tight that I remembered my nails digging into him and I had to force myself to let go. I then leaned into his chest again to feel and smell him; it was so hard to breathe. I had to pull away, but the tears kept coming in waves. Once the calmness took over after about an hour, he then removed himself to go to bed. I felt emotionally wiped out!

The next morning there was a change in him, a quiet and profound disconnect, more pronounced than ever before. He was going away on business the following day and I was at work, so I did not see him leave at 3am. His parting text just read "Have a good week".

8 days went by and he never texted me once that week!

During that week, I went to see a Lawyer who advised me that our pot of money was small and that I should screw him for the lot! The second lawyer told me the same and that the court would require 3-5 years of maintenance because of our differing earning potential. I came away from those meetings with such a mixture of relief, anger and a hatred for what our marriage and life had become.

After a few days pondering this, I have to add it was all I could do not to call him, I realised that this mess we had both created was exactly that: our mess, not my fault nor his. Equal opportunity dumpster fire!

During our marriage, I had not been aware of his inability to be a good friend to me nor anyone else in his life. This realisation came so much later. If it is a work relationship he had to build or contend with, he will read every self-help/business book on the market to make that work, not in the personal arena though. One of his oldest friends, I would now say, is one of my closest male friends. He has such amazing insight into 'us' and is the only person who really tells me the 100% ugly truth, and I treasure that.

For his family, I was the bridge builder there too. I worry that he will isolate himself, but I have to learn to stop worrying about him and his future, because I am damn sure he has barely given me a second thought these last few years!

So, dating sites! During a particularly sad and lonely Saturday night, with a plate of cheese and crackers, two bottles of Shiraz and some Sade playing, I joined three different dating sites. Wow, it is indeed a strangely insane world we now live in. On one of these sites my age preference was 45-55 but it seems like I was getting 'dick pics' from the strangest 50+ year old men who looked more like 65-70 to me! On another site, two men asked me if I was willing to be their submissive. And on the third site, there was a proposition of sex with the finale of cum shot and a $100 bonus for my trouble. I think I may suspend my accounts for a foreseeable—or maybe not!

Out of nowhere there was this one man who popped up with a twinkle in his eye whom I was drawn to, so I messaged him. He got back to me and we texted a lot over the next three days whilst he was travelling from the UK to Perth. He sent me videos of him in first class, we shared stories of picture postcard winters evening activities, whether we loved mountains or beaches, the music we were listening to; he also showed me a picture of his house on the beach and we shared what was happening in our respective failed marriages. Apparently, a three-day online relationship is a thing now. As soon as he arrived home again it was radio silence! Oh well! It was fun while it lasted.

He was supposed to come home from a business trip today, and what just dawned on me right now is that, he does not give me a second thought in anything he does; no update on plans, no flight details, no, "honey I am home" nothing. I am trying to think back to a time that he did do that and sadly, I cannot recall; it must be years! I had a little cry, then got mad at myself because I have to learn to not care and try to disconnect from this. It is hard for me to admit that I still want the best for him and that I care, and he does not feel the same way.

I sent an email to him once he did arrive home to ask him for a chat to go over what the Lawyers had told me. I am grinding my teeth trying to stay civil! I told him what I expected and when I said 3-5 years maintenance, I saw his eyebrows rise as if to say that isn't going to happen. I told him I needed a life insurance policy, as there is no retirement plan and he did not like the sound of that either! He said he would reach out to his Lawyer to get some info and get back to me in a few days—So another four days of silence which I have learned is normal 'processing time' for him and he did agree to 60% of our pot and a life insurance, but needed more time to ponder on the maintenance.

Off he goes again this week to France on business. I was glad to see him go if I am honest. After an excruciating week of him being sick with a cold, coughing and sniffing and groaning like the "man-flu" is the end of the world!

After a lovely alone week of planning my escape and starting to pack, sadly he was home again and I heard him receive a call from an Executive Coach he had used in the US. And he lamented to him about loving Europe and travelling around and the pace of life here? I am hard pressed to understand his version of his life and the reality of living his life. His version is an exciting life of jet setting around Europe meeting people and conducting business. But the reality is, him getting up at stupid O'clock, working online before work, going to work and then after work doing work/emails, eating, emailing whilst eating, going to his hotel and going to bed around 7-8pm, wash and repeat!! Sad really to think of all the places we have travelled together and he has never really 'seen' any of them. I realised long ago that if I did not make my own plans, I would sit in a hotel room waiting for him to come back to go to sleep, so I no longer waited toward our end, I would go so I could travel and do local tours, catch local buses, go on boat tours and experience life in all the wonderful places. I appreciate him for those experiences. Sadly, in the last three years we have not even shared the same hotel rooms because of his sleep patterns.

If I am honest, I truly have a lot to be thankful for, but as most separated/divorced women will attest, this whole process is soul crushing, weight loss inspiring, eye opening, red flag defining and life changing in every single way.

I am annoyed at myself for not requiring change sooner. When I did require it, I am furious at myself for accepting the 7-10-day turnaround to 'the norm' again. What in the hell was I thinking?

All these things are sent to teach us boundaries. It is just a little frustrating that it takes maturity and years of experience before we 'get it!'

After a particularly harrowing week where he was away with work and I had to view four absolutely horrible flats that cost ¾ of my monthly pay and ⅓ of the size of where I had lived the last 20+ years, I was feeling destitute and more nervous about where I would end up and whether living in a broom closet would be worth it for my peace of mind!

It seemed all I wanted to do is engage him in some way so to see if he was feeling as lost as I was, but I resisted.

Strangely enough, I received a message from him the following morning that read, "I feel broken by this whole thing," so I offered to meet for dinner because I feel strongly that I do not want to destroy him anymore than he already is, so we went for dinner. He was nervous and it showed by his hands shaking and I was nervous driving from work as I had butterflies! We sat by the window in a restaurant in town and I ordered some stilton and pitta bread and a drink. After a couple of bites, I had a super strong piece of cheese, so I instinctively said, "Ew" and handed the bread half eaten to him and he just popped it in his mouth, like we had never missed a beat or said "Divorce!"

The next day after work I suggested we go to the cinema so we went to see Downton Abbey. Afterwards, whilst driving home I asked him, "What is important to you?"

The five hours that followed sitting in the car was real, raw, honest, tearful, and eye opening. He admitted he was a broken man, and he had unplugged before me. He admitted he was an awful husband and dad, and that the Company I already mentioned prior had 'broken him'. He said that after selling his soul there that he literally had nothing to give at the end of the day; he admitted that the move to an out-of-town job/apartment was a big mistake; he said that the red flags are so great even at the job where he is now. He said when his personal life spirals out of control he just plugs into work for validation.

At the end of that revelation I said again, "What is important?" and he said he did not know anymore. I took my right hand and put it on his thigh and I took my left hand and put it on my heart and said, "this/us is—what is important?" Our family is what is important, not the job, not the money, not all the stuff but US! What 'we' had is what was important to me and asked if it was important to him and his reply was "Yes, it is all that is important."

I asked him to look at me and I said, "Here is my offer. I will stay with you whilst you get the emotional help that you need from the counsellor we were seeing together. If you need

19

three sessions a week for three months then do that, get your anxiety under control and find a solution for your sleep issue. I offered to just support him till he feels like he is not imploding."

The next week was full of plans for Christmas Holidays, Thoughts of moving jobs, asking about me sleeping in the same room and one awfully emotional try at sex, it was pained, forced and when he had finished there were more tears.

I had ordered him some CBD gummies for sleep and some St. John's Wort for mood elevation, as suggested by our counsellor. He is still drinking way too much, still eating junk food, and still leaving at 5am when he does rarely go to work! He is still going to bed between 7-8pm too. After this emotional week he informed me tonight that he cannot feel anything for me and doesn't know if he ever can. I informed him yet again that it took six plus years to drive this into the ditch and it will take more than six days to resurrect it, to which he nodded. I told him 'I' am not the reason this is in the ditch, and we are the causality of his unravelling and also that I am just here to support him and the relationship is not even an issue right now, that getting him emotionally stable again is.

I was talking to our/my good male friend today who questioned my ability to be able to blow up this relationship bridge, and that what I am doing is the opposite of divorce. My only reaction to that, right now, is that he is destroyed and I would feel awful if he did something to himself and I did not try to help him. I do feel like 'I' am not his answer. He cannot make himself happy right now and he certainly could not make me happy. This is fooking exhausting! So, I shall start looking again for jobs, I think. I see this ending still, and I will not live the rest of my life with a sad/broken man that has admitted that when he looks at me, which is not very often, all he sees is his own failures. How dare he? I am so much better than this.

I think there is something to be said about 'Male Menopause'. Their hormones fluctuate just like women's hormones do, and they have awakenings too. Parents dying/Jobs changing or jobs not being satisfying, marriages ending/kids leaving home. I just think that maybe 'back in the day' men just went to the pub, plugged in at work more, played darts or football and that was how they got through that, and most women did not require change from their men but we are in a different world now. He said to me during a text message today, "I am sorry, I shall try to man up!" which made me really sad. How awful to have to live in a world/environment where feeling something is still seen as a male failure or weakness! I feel so sad for him.

Here we are still talking about him, his feelings, his job, his future, his sadness and nothing has changed just like I anticipated. He is still drinking a lot, still not really interacting with me nor his Friends, not doing any counselling. Last night he was in bed by 6.45 and tonight by 7.20.

He texted me at work today and apologised for it being a bad day yesterday, although I am not really sure why it was a bad day as all this exhausting emotional turmoil seems to be melding into a fuzzy every day normality now! He asked me to go to dinner so I asked him to pick a place. Two hours later he hadn't, so I messaged him and arranged the same place we had gone two weeks prior and he agreed. So, I drive up and he is talking on the phone in his car and signals that he will be there in one minute. I go in, get a table and a drink and sit and wait. This was a red flag for me that something else was happening now, He came in 10 minutes later, I did not ask who he was talking to but he shared that it was his sister, I am still so disappointed in his inability to put me first. He has been alone at home all day! couldn't he have called whoever he was talking to earlier? I am mad at myself that I keep putting myself through this! He does not understand my perspective at all, even though I keep explaining it to him. I told him that I was at work, you could not put me first for an hour or so?! He retorted "I am always making you so angry and you are always disappointed in me." I just sat for a second and stared out the window while he continued to play the Victim card. I looked at him and turned and asked the waiter for the check and turned back to him and stated "I am worth so much more than this. I want a man who wants to be with me, wants to laugh, wants to be with me sexually wants to be my friend and supports me." He looked shocked almost like it was the first time I had said this! I got up and put my coat on to leave, he walked out first and we did not speak.

I got in my car and him in his, as he left straight away and I just sat there listening to some music. After sometime I decided to just drive and see where I end up. 10 minutes later he called and asked me to come home to talk. I pulled over to weigh my feelings and my choices and damper my butterflies. How many cycles of this will there be before he decides it is enough, and then I can leave with a clear conscience? Why do I care—Why can't I just end it, why?

My next question in my irrational mind is, "Why can't I have my cake and eat it too?" Why can't I stay here where it's comfortable and have a relationship outside of this! Why can't

I get what I need from multiple people? Why do I have to abide by society's 'Norm'? Why is it all or nothing? Can't I make my own rules as long as I'm not lying 'lying by omission'? Why can't I make him happy by staying and make myself happy and meet someone who makes me laugh and have amazing sex?

Speaking of said aforementioned mad idea, I have started looking on dating apps again as I am still lonely and alone a lot. Match.com matched me with an Irish guy. We met for coffee one morning and he was quick witted, sexy, expressive, interested, introspective, and open about his past relationships and his life experiences. I was honest about everything, however, he did not ask about divorce. We hung out, had tea, shared life experiences and shared a little kiss. He walked me back to my car and I came back home. I left him to ponder 'me' a little, and thought he would say "You are looking for more than I am willing to give" but instead he gave the mansplaining version of that which is "Let's be FWB and see if it progresses." He did however go on to admit that he does not want me to sleep with anyone else, and that he wants to take ownership of me in the bedroom and eventually he wants me to find another woman to fulfil his lifelong fantasy of a threesome; so some things for me to ponder, not!

Meanwhile on the Homefront, he has progressed along like the 'Divorce' word was never spoken. He has not called to sort out more counselling; is still drinking too much, never looks at me and still goes off and does his own thing without giving me a thought. However, he does want to go away over Xmas, so he booked us a seven-day holiday. I have zero idea what he is thinking, and sharing a room with him? He cannot even look at me anymore. I feel bad for him and spend too much time taking the blame to make him feel better. I am feeling this will of course come to a head, and I should make a sodding decision, but I still feel so torn!

I came home from work today and he had made me dinner which was a lovely, however, he did not eat with me or sit with me. After I ate, I thanked him and told him how much I appreciated the thought—30 minutes later at 7pm he was in bed!! Sadly, he is like a 75-year-old man with his strange routines.

Got home after work the following day and he had already started drinking early in the day, and it looks like he is watching football and was on his phone so I came upstairs to leave him to it, before the incessant drunken babbling that always happens begins! Sadly when he drinks he goes to bed ridiculously early and then wakes up at everyone else's regular bedtime, and then is up all night long walking the hallways like an elephant, stomping around the house vibrating the floorboards like the loud voices in my mind saying "stay and try to help him", "go now and never see him again," "feel bad for him and then fook this!!"

When I came down in the morning he was a crying, tired wreck. He decided to go to McDonald's so I took my chance to get out for a run. I got changed and left right as he was coming back. He looked shocked that I was going out so I only got around the block before I felt so bad that I had to come back. We sat in silence till he went back to bed at 10am!! This is torture. I still think he feels like I am the answer to his happiness, but he is not the answer to mine. Am I heartless or is his mental state affecting my rational mind? It's almost like an emotional control he has over me.

All I know is, he does not want to be with me. This feels too much like hard work, and I want, need and deserve someone who wants to be with me. I want to feel butterflies about my partner, currently I just feel sick about this situation. This is not a soft or safe place for me and has not been for a really long time! My question to myself has to reverberate through the walls, "How am I going to get out of here? When will we call time?" "Why can't I call it!?"

I bought tickets to go see Russell Brand in his 12-step program, he asked if he could come with me even though I knew it was not his kind of thing, it was in Slough of all places! I have to say that Russell was amazing, I welled up a few times, he looked deep into all of our souls that night and struck so many chords within me, also clarifying for me that I am the only person that can make myself happy and that it is not my job to make him happy, whole nor complete— liberating! He is the least spiritually connected person I know, although with his state of mind I suppose that is to be expected. Look, why am I making excuses!!

He informed me this week that he needs to make his own path, and I am getting whiplash from this tennis match of emotions, back and forth and always on his terms! He did say he was going to cancel the holiday he bought for us and I told him that I am not going to sit here over Christmas, so I am going to go alone—to which he looked shocked!

Another week went by with not much talking nor any interaction till Wednesday. And there comes an email from his Attorney with an attached financial settlement: a kick to the gut that literally took my breath away! He did not want to give me more than three years of maintenance/alimony, no pension sharing, and lucky me, I get to keep my car!

I was so shocked; it was lucky I was at work so it had a chance to sit and simmer within me. I checked our joint account and he had moved half our money out of it, and when he got paid the next day, he took a big chunk of money out to put in his new bank account that he has set up for himself. I tried to message him and he had blocked me, so I emailed him to ask him to talk because we need to figure out how we can work through this as the bills have to get paid. To which his reply was, "You took your pay check out of the account and I did not know what you were doing so—" I informed him that I did not get paid until the day after tomorrow! So, he admitted that he was unaware, and then he disappeared for 48 hours to a hotel somewhere and according to the online banking, watched Amazon Prime videos!! He is like a passive aggressive petulant child!

After such a stressful week and knowing him so well, I realised that there is no way he will part with the most precious thing in his life without a fight, so fight we shall!

The Attorney will answer his 'proposal' with a kind 'Hell No,' and we shall see where we go from here. Admittedly I am nervous, sick to my stomach and constantly on edge. This is not good for my health and my blood pressure is through the roof again. Yet his way of dealing with things is to drink prosecco in his room and order vibrators (?), and shop like everything is just the same in his world! Whereas in reality, I now realise things are just the same for him as the only change now is that he does not have to pretend anymore. He can just go on with his life as always.

He really brings out the very worst in me. If I had a friend going through this, I would go over and help her pack her stuff and make her stay with me. I need to hold out till the financial stuff is sorted though. He goes from texting me when he is bored to ignoring me for days on end! It is literally emotional torture being here.

I was looking up the Holiday villa he had booked for us over Christmas and was getting quite excited about getting away. I checked for my passport in my files and mysteriously it had disappeared. I stayed up till 3am and tore the house apart looking for it and yes you guessed it, nowhere to be found! He denied he had seen it but I know him!

I then went about the business of cancelling my passport and he went about the business of cancelling the holiday he paid 3600 for and got 300 back—alarm bells are ringing!

He left for a two-week business trip in Prague yesterday.

I had a date from Match.com; his profile showed a super cute looking 6'2" guy, with beautiful eyes. I drove the half hour to the gorgeous little pub he had picked, we sat down and he got me a half of cider and a pint for himself. We talked about Christmas, lone travel, his daughter, his favourite food and after 55 minutes he called time, so I drove home really disappointed. I was at the very least hoping to have a mad sexual encounter but apparently "I was a bit too flat and laid back" for him! He was nowhere near 6'2" either. I felt sorry for myself for the rest of the night, then pulled myself together the next morning and reminded myself that I do not need a man to rescue me, and right then and there I decided that I am never going to be able to find everything in one man, and that I should just stop looking for that! Maybe it can be alright to have a different man for different things—sex, travel, shopping, conversation, why can't I do that? Why isn't that socially acceptable?

He has been gone for a week now and I have to be honest that I have seen and felt a big shift. I feel like he does not play into my decisions anymore, a feeling of disconnect and even two days went by that I did not even think about him. I have been pretty busy with work, doing classes at the gym and talking to my kids most days too, and of course writing this book is literally pouring out of me.

I completed a new will this week too which I have to be honest and say felt liberating. I will have nothing to give but it felt nice to just get my own stuff sorted. The new passport I applied for is no longer as Mrs. but as a Ms., and that felt good too!

Went and met my financial advisor this afternoon to ask advice about this Split Dollar Life Insurance Policy he has. It does say all over the paperwork that there is a surrender value which would allow me to buy a small house, and it means that I would not be sitting up at 3am writing this roller coaster of a story wondering how in the hell am I actually going to be able to financially survive for the rest of my life!

I feel strangely really angry today that he has spent 20+ years berating his other family members behind their backs, for the bad financial decisions they have made, yet here we are! He keeps reminding me that he has no legacy, making it sound like I have spent a huge amount of money: Then I discover there is no money! I am not the one with a hoarding/shopping issue! I am shocked that I have left myself in this predicament and that I should have forced him to do a pension and a will and let me see all this stuff he was doing. Hindsight is 20/20 though, and now I see why he was always stalling!

After a stressful 10 days at work, my Boss's has discovered his wife has multiple cancers, his/their world is unravelling, and I am conscious though of his obvious love and adoration for her. Who does not want that! All these things are a reminder of what I have not had for a really long time.

I decided to go down to the coast for Christmas time. I know I cannot sit in the house with him for a full weekend, never mind 10 days. Strange though that he ignores me whilst I am at home but as soon as I leave, he then texts me—control or loneliness I do wonder, "Where is this and that, we need to talk."

I drove down by the coast for Christmas with my family. I got some great seafront runs in and also some clifftop crying and screaming too!

I got up today after an amusing meeting last night with my very first boyfriend Gary from when I was 16 years old. Our relationship was less about my first sexual experience, as that was less than memorable, and more about learning to be out from my Parent's house. We were more party couple and less about the relationship stuff. Anyway I digress, facially he looked exactly the same but of course he is closer to 60 than 50 and it showed on his face. He was not a smoker back then but is now, still drinking 'snakebite' after 30 years, and I am surprised his liver still works. It seems Gary never really progressed in his life and has not grown emotionally, and he had a thinning man bun! After one drink I took him to where all my family were finishing off dinner and subjected him to them all night. He bought me two drinks for the entire night and I bought the rest. At the end of the night someone in the family called a taxi for us all and apparently, he had said to my sister he was going to walk me home, to which my sister replied "No you are not. She's getting a taxi home with us!" My family tolerated him and were very welcoming but I have to be honest and say, I will never hear the end of that, and the jokes will be relentless.

Sitting here now after getting up before sunrise to go run on the beach was an amazing feeling. Newquay is the most beautiful place, and I would love to live here. I am filling out the Financial Statement for my lawyers, which is due in 10 days. I am realising that the lifestyle I used to have will be no more and I have no idea how he is going to make his life work financially either. I simply have to stop thinking about him.

There is however an impending welling of excitement within me which is still manifesting as tears on a regular basis—maybe grieving, maybe a mixture.

Today is Christmas Day and my first one in 30+ years where I am alone and definitely feel it, even though I am surrounded by my family. I think I cried three times yesterday and lost count of how many times I held back tears. My kids are all in the USA and they are all alright. I understand my emotions are about the change in me.

I had a dream last night that my soon to be ex meets someone. She is younger and prettier and she will have a child or two, but that is when he will need to feel wanted. He needs a person with no idea of how his narcissism manifests, hence the younger woman, seems like that is the way of the 'Midlife Crisis'.

I got home from my emotional trip to the mundane. The bins were not out, the house was a mess, and he was drunk and locked in the living room. Strangely the texts whilst I was away that "we need to talk" did not manifest at all. Just like magic he gets up in the morning, goes to McDonalds then disappears overnight. Just reminds me that nothing has nor will ever change with him.

Tinder dating: Talking on Tinder is like sifting through the worst of humanity. Then there is the odd one that stands out. I have been talking to a 'Dominic' in air quotes because a lot of the time their names online are not real. Three days in, which apparently seems like a lifetime in the dating stratosphere, we had covered a lot of ground: Family, Life, Spirituality, religion, life goals and priorities and the fact that he sold everything and lives on a boat near Southampton. We agreed initially to meet halfway but on reflection, I pondered that if I really liked him and whether he was going to break my 'dry spell'. I would need a few drinks and agreed to meet him in his local pub. So, a 40-minute drive of nerves was all it took to get to our 2pm meeting.

I arrived early, as I tend to always do, and he walked in and I could not read his facial expressions, but one drink in he told me he was pleasantly surprised as the ethereal light behind the bar shone and lit my beauty! To which I rolled my eyes and I said 'Bullshit!' We both laughed. We went for a walk around Hamble, he put his arm around me and we walked toward the harbour. He propositioned me for a hug which felt warm and real and I had to resist the urge to cry. In that moment he looked down at me and said, "This is your first hug outside your marriage, isn't it?" It was hard to hold back the tears and I just held him close as to not look at him. When I did release him, he leaned in and kissed my cold nose then a peck on my lips; so sweet, tender and lovely.

I agreed to go back to his boat and I was a little nervous walking through town but I came all this way and decided to brave my insecurities. After climbing aboard he showed me all the work he had done to his new home and he started to unpack the shopping he had done earlier that day. In the bag was an Amazon package, which said, "Make yourself useful and open this." Inside fell out a packet of KY jelly and some bike lights. He was SO embarrassed and I put aside my nervousness again and spotted a bread knife on the draining board and told him that it was only a cartwheel and an elbow to the nether regions away, and we both laughed. He offered me a drink and I refused just in case I still had to drive home. He admitted that he had to eat because he is Type 1 Diabetic, so I ate raw carrots whilst he made spaghetti with pesto for himself. The conversation flowed as the wood burner warmed the small space we sat in. He ate and after he asked for a cuddle, so we sat and continued talking. He said, "You are a delicate flower that needs plucking one petal at a time, aren't you?" I pondered why that made me angry, and then I sat up off his chest and said "I am not a delicate flower in any aspect of my life, and you need to know that." I maybe a little soft and gooey on the inside but never delicate, I thought that was enough of a 'real' moment for now and leaned back into the cuddle again. Thinking about what was just said I got up again and kissed him, it started slow and had maybe too much tongue for me. I tried to lead him, then I felt the change in him as he got a little more aggressive, he put his hands in my hair. It was passionate and it felt lovely to be wanted. He then went for the boob grab so I stopped him and knew then I was not going to sleep with him at least not tonight. He walked me back up to the Marina to my car and I drove home. I woke up and it was New Year's Day. I felt a pang of guilt and I wanted to hug my soon to be Ex! After a little ponder, I reminded myself that this last year has been really difficult and all the talk of 'New Year' is the reason I was feeling a little down. So here I am writing my feelings down.

It is really hard for me and my personality type to be in limbo. I hope that in the next couple of months clarity will emerge but for right now, here I sit pondering, hoping, winging it and writing!

Today I sit on my lunch break at work. The date is Jan 3rd, and my Boss's wife has just been admitted to Hospice care after only being diagnosed on Dec 20th. He said that she went from being the absolute love of his life, she was horse riding three weeks ago to now not being able to sit up in bed. It took me back to a place in my mind, which does not seem that long ago, when I described my relationship as this "I feel completely worshipped by him, I am his everything and he makes me feel that every single day." How cruel and awful the hands of time can be! Now I feel like the passion I had for him and us has become this parasite, eating away at what feels like my "goodness". I feel like he makes me the very worst version of myself.

It is Sunday morning and I get back from the gym. He has been acting stranger than normal and could not even look me in the face yesterday or today. I felt a total shift within him. When I got back from a run, he was upstairs, I went upstairs to strip my bed. I got sucked into a rabbit hole on my phone, I sat down in my bedroom, then I hear him talking in a different tone, not a work or family or kid call. So, I stood by my door and heard the word 'Babe' coming out of his mouth. My heart was beating out of my chest and so I continued to listen. I was transfixed to the spot not able to hear anything but his voice and my heartbeat in my head. He was saying,

"Didn't you enjoy our days together Friday and Saturday?" Her reply, "I am not sure if it is over for you and your wife," he replied with "Oh it is, after what she just said today." This poor woman probably spent two days with him whilst he showed off with his BMW, money, motorbikes and expensive hotel overnight stays whilst he just bashed me and our marriage and made himself the victim in this. She was making an excuse about having an upset stomach. Sounds to me like she was saying 'thanks for the ride but you are not ready for a relationship yet'. The problem with a narcissist is that they cannot hear the other person, it is only what they want to hear. After his call, I opened his door and just said

"Perfect."

"What is," was his reply.

"Babe," I replied. He followed me downstairs and he was mortified that I had caught him in the act. He made excuses then went into full on 'victim'.

"You are going to take everything from me. I have worked my whole life to end up with nothing. You never made me feel wanted or appreciated or loved." Sadly my next action was so childish, I picked up my half full cold mug of tea and threw it at him, but it hit the door not him. We were both shocked at my action. Divorce by its very nature is absolute madness. He then said. "He has no one here and that he needed to find someone to connect and talk too."

I replied, "But my family and friends and kids have reached out to you and you have ignored them." His Friends in the US have tried too and nothing either. It's like literally fighting with a toddler who says "Yeah but—" after everything you say.

After a couple of hours, I had cooled down. I realised that although I was angry, he had just done the same thing as me. I could not physically be with anyone yet but we are different people. He is just trying to get through this the best he can with his limited emotional capabilities, and it was another stark reminder that I dislike him as a person and I no longer actively love him.

Thank you universe, I appreciate the extra shove.

After a restless night I woke with a strange new defiance and can actually now see, feel, smell and taste my future without him, and I am excited about that possibility.

It had been a rough few weeks at work. My Bosses wife passed away and my strange witchy powers told me that morning that she passed. Sounds strange to say but I have always felt this 'Gift' but fought it till I was in my mid-30s. Now I embrace it; I have a sense for death and also for pregnancy. Sad that from my Boss's wife's diagnosis to passing was 22 days. Shocking really!

I have been having my own private struggle with a health issue too, but I put that on the back burner whilst all this other stuff was going on.

Today I went to the Doctors as I have been having some bleeding. I knew this was not normal as I have had a partial hysterectomy. The Dr talked about STDs and my brain started reeling, could he, would he, did he? I told her it had been months since I have last had intercourse and she said, "Let's take a look and take some swabs." She called for a chaperone and I disrobed. She did the swabs and asked if it was alright to take a look. I agreed and she said that she could see what looked like a tampon string. I told her that is not possible as it's been eight years since I last had a period. She suggested that she can pull it to see what it is. As she did, a sharp pain seared through me like a hot poker and I recoiled. She apologised and then she said "I think it is a loose stitch from your hysterectomy and I will need to refer you to a Gynaecologist to have that snipped, trimmed or removed." My head is still reeling from the STD revelation, and so I returned home to find him gone off to wherever he sleeps now. I took some pain meds and went to the gym and did a class to work out some pent-up anger. Yet, here I sit at 1am writing and I am wondering who will be able to drive me back from the hospital after this procedure? The following week I arrived at the Hospital, Pre-op appointment, to see the doctor and she was very abrupt and emotionless. She advised me to undress and 'relax' as she prodded and poked and swabbed around inside of me. Afterwards I dressed as she advised me, "the stitch is not what is causing the bleeding but I could not see what is there. However, the swab showed there is some blood there, so maybe an ulcer—but I need to put you under to see and I shall cut the stitch as well as it may cause issues when/if you do become sexually active again." I got a little upset as I do not want to go under anaesthesia if I can help it!

I left there thinking I did not want her to do it even if I do have it done. I drove home as I had agreed to talk to the soon to be ex and try to figure a way forward as the Lawyers are all in it for the cash. We talked for an hour or so. We talked about when we both thought it went wrong. He said "I never appreciated him" and I said "he never noticed me," he said "I unplugged" and I said "he filled his life with stuff instead of me", so, "He said, she said" Seriously though, separation literally makes fools out of us!

I told him I was going to the Doctor's tonight. He did not inquire how I was feeling nor how it went. It just reminded me that he does not care about anyone but himself. I went to bed a little while after and cried harder that I have cried for a long time. I feel so very alone and unsupported.

Who will drive me to the hospital and back? Who is my next of kin now?

I spent the next few days wishing for a bygone time where I was adored, nurtured, cared for and appreciated.

He became really sick with the 'Man flu'. I texted to ask if he needed anything and to remind him to hydrate and medicate to get his temperature down, and still nothing in return. No texts saying, "Heard from the Dr or the hospital?" Then right at the time I normally leave work, I get a text of an offer for financial settlement. What the actual hell! He literally cannot think about anyone but himself! Why don't I listen to my own advice ever? When people show you who they are, believe them! Why can't I actually believe what an awful Human he is! Looks like I shall just have to be real about the lone life that I shall be living from here on out.

This last week of turmoil has been the final awakening. It has shown me that he cannot care about anyone but himself. His body language and response proved that when I asked about his infidelity, also his lack of care about my current medical challenges: all this was the final slap upside the head for me.

I told my work colleagues what was going on and I got a cuddle from my boss who just reminded me that my soon to be ex must just be a bastard. He said, "All we want at times like these is someone to hold/cuddle us." He is exactly right. That is all we need: understanding, support and love.

Woke up early today and texted another offer of financial support so we shall see what he thinks.

We texted back and forth whilst I was at work until I noticed the tone in his text change, which always signalled there was alcohol involved. He then becomes the victim, "You did this, I am in turmoil, I cannot breathe," I then have to stop and leave him be, although this is really hard for me. I am instinctually kind hearted even though I have been destroyed by this person over and over again! If this was a Friend/Relative I would never allow them to treat me this way. My bullshit meter is broken or faulty when it comes to him, but also realizing that this is all about control for him and I have to 'play nice' till the divorce is sorted out.

When I opened my computer to write today, there were lots of pages left open. He had been looking on my computer and I do not know what he was looking for but luckily this was not something he had read. Although all this is true and this could have been brutal for him to relive, I am sure.

Latest dating update: Met in person with a guy I had been talking to on Match.com, Gary. Not my normal type at all, but his profile was insightful, funny and real and showed an emotional intelligence that stood out from the rest. He was blond, fair skinned and flashy in his style but oh my, his voice and sense of humour took over, and he smelled so great. We met at 6.15 and talked till 10.15. There was laughing, real moments about how he became a widow; funny stories of travels we both had, spirituality and conspiracy theories, motivational people we follow. I wanted to invite him back as he held my face and came in for a tender little kiss and I was frozen to the spot for a millisecond. We texted 'Goodnight' and 'Good Morning' and then nothing so we shall see what transpires. He has an intense career, two kids, an Au Pair so busy—busy. Would be nice but in reality, maybe too early for me anyway. A week goes by and nothing so just another one-off date.

Slowly packing up my whole life into boxes, I am selling some big furniture too, as I am realising that all this 'stuff' my soon to be ex is emotionally attached to, will bring me nothing but bad memories.

He is in the US currently and I need to get out of the house before he returns in three weeks. He said that he did not believe I would be gone when he returned. I of course took that as a challenge! He is sorting his work visa in the US and barely hanging out with the kids; not seeing his friends but staying with his sister which is good. We have actually talked on the phone since he has been in the US. He still is all about how bad he feels and how broken he is but I have felt the need to keep it all civil and light till the maintenance thing is signed sealed and delivered. Then I think I am going to have to cut him off for a few months as I need to heal. This rollercoaster of emotions is brutal.

So Valentine's Day, what would have been our 21st Wedding Anniversary today, it seems every song I hear makes me want to rock and cry in a corner. It got so bad at work today that I had to leave at lunchtime so I could cry and walk as I could not seem to hold it in.

I reached out to him and he said he felt just as bad. Yet, he talked and talked about how I made him feel like he was never good enough and that he was never appreciated. He said that he was not broken and that if he fell off the planet tomorrow, no one would notice, to which I told him that he has to learn how to connect and build friendships, but again, he doesn't think he is ever in the wrong so it fell on deaf ears!

A few hours later and it seems that he was listening to music on iTunes and downloaded 40 songs out of our account. Priorities, I suppose!

Today I received the next Lawyer instalment and to say it was like a truck hit me would be an understatement! He has filed for divorce and he wants me to pay half the costs for it. He always wants me to pay for half his move out costs and he gave the reasons for the breakdown of the marriage:

"Over the last four years the Petitioner has become emotionally distant. She has ceased spending time and engaging in connected activities such as running, going to the gym and motorcycle riding"—All of which we have done.

Over the past four years the Respondent has not shown the Petitioner any love or affection, and we were still having sex till around three months ago.

He states that I persuaded him to liquidate everything he has spent on our whole marriage together building, and move back to the UK. We decided together to leave the US together for so many reasons: His parents passing away, wanting a simpler life, our daughters' medical issues, the POTUS.

He stated that I have not integrated him in my family since we have been back in the Country. He has come to every family event we have aside from my last Christmas trip to Newquay.

He also stated that during our Marriage, I called him names and said he was an inadequate partner, friend, husband and father—all those things are in fact true unfortunately. He said that I have affected his self-esteem and he is now taking antidepressants and doing counselling. I have to admit that when I read all of this, it was all I could do to get my coat on and leave work before I literally fell to bits on a walk. I called him and told him that I literally felt devastated by his comments. He got upset too and he said that he actually feels all the things he wrote.

Sadly the only thing divorce breeds is rich Lawyers hatred and resentment between Partners. I feel sick to my stomach and so tense I could scream, cry or spontaneously combust at different points during the same day! I left work that day feeling exhausted and broken. I got home, changed, went to the gym crank out a mile sprint and a class. I slept well that night!

Hospital Day: I awoke early at around 4.15am. I have a cab booked at 6am to get to the Hospital to have this long suture and the two polyps removed. I was nervous about going. The Hospital was not happy about the lone Taxi ride there alone nor returning home alone either. All that emotional anticipation of the general anaesthetics was outweighed by the daily smack upside the head that reminds me I am alone. My life scares me the sadness hits me like a damn tidal wave some days, and other days I do not even think of him—Progress I suppose and understanding that it is a process.

Today was waves of dreading but also a strong realisation that I have to find my purpose, that there just has to be meaning and growth to this pain. I have to get through this with a goal or what's the point? After this phase I have to move toward an advocate purpose: to share knowledge and wisdom and make those around me realise what is real.

The cycle of a text every three days arrived to ask me "What is the Lawyer update?" I informed him that there isn't an update. He replied, "I am sorry, but I am emotionally spent, I am in hell and I cannot move forward with a new life after the old one has been swept away: I am stuck in purgatory." Wow, he really does keep showing/telling me that he does not care about anyone but his own feelings and self-doubt, and I just keep expecting a different outcome. Divorce is truly the definition of absolute madness!

I get a strange text from him asking, "I hope you are alright. Do you need someone to go with you to your appointment on Friday?" I informed him, "I appreciate it, but no thank you!" and my thinking was correct, it was not about caring as he went ahead that day and filed the divorce papers to the Court.

I am full on into the Dating Apps again which are honestly like a minefield of speed dating and a whole relationship in a day: elation, learning, disappointment then ghosting! I suppose it saves and kills some time.

So, today was the day of my test results. I had not heard from him at all today. I did however here from my Lawyer who stated that because he has filed divorce papers in court before the financial stuff was sorted that now I will be in limbo with no maintenance until the Decree Nisi is done, so 3-6 months! I did make a decision that if he did not reach out to check on me or maybe turn up at my appointment, I'd block him totally. My appointment was at 6.30 pm and the all the tests came back negative. I reached out to thank all the people who have supported me during the last two weeks of added turmoil and heard nothing from him, so I blocked him from contacting me. I had to do that for my mental well-being. He will think I'll reach out to ask for money and interact but I cannot. I will have to just stay put here till all the Divorce stuff is sorted.

After a week of 'settling in' with the test results, I had prepared for either scenario with a contingency plan for both. What it did show me was that I had to block him from being able to contact me in any way; so block him I did! The first week was the hardest but the more days that go by the easier it gets. Two weeks on and a couple of whole days have passed without me thinking about him for more than a minute or two.

The Coronavirus has shut down the World and my drive to pursue Life Coaching has never been stronger. I have offered some free sessions to people to get some experiences and recommendations too.

My last day of work due to Covid shutdowns was today and I am looking forward to getting some running in, get a business name, plan and site started. I watched a ton of Ted Talks, read and prepared for my goal and made a plan for the rest of this year.

I got some gardening done: running, cleaning and reading too. I saw him drive by whilst I was out running yesterday. I received the current attorney letter today stating that he does not want to talk about the financial stuff until two months from now as he feels his job is in jeopardy because of the Coronavirus. I emailed him and asked him to call me. He called me within five minutes and said it was nice to see me yesterday and I pretended I did not see him. He said that he had texted and emailed me multiple times. I told him I had blocked him as it was too hard to be connected for me. He went on to tell me about his sadness, his worry about his job situation and his way forward. He asked me about my job and who I was talking to and I just turned the conversation back into his issues. He cried twice and I tried to help him see perspective and take one issue at a time as he has always struggled to do that.

When I woke up today, I spent the morning talking to the important people in my life that needed support, and I get a text from him telling me he loved me. I just replied with "Please call". To which he replied that he was on a conference call till later in the day, so I just ended the conversation with "OK". I went on with my day in isolation, which I have to admit I am enjoying very much right now.

He texted me around 3pm asking if he could call; I was out running so I contemplated ignoring him, but I answered and agreed. He said he was out walking around the city centre and said he had a confession to make. I laughed and said "Do tell". He said that he was so very sorry, and I said, "Just tell me". He said, I have made a complete mess for myself and I said "say it!" He admitted that he has moved in with someone that has a 10-year-old kid. I must admit I just start laughing; he asked where you are right now and I told him I was right by that awful pub near our old house that we had a few awful meetings at. He said "wait there and I will come to you," so wait I did.

He turned up on his Harley and just stared at me and burst into tears, and I again started laughing. I told him I knew him better than he knows himself and that I had called this and how predictable he was. He said for someone so smart he does some dumb shite and I replied "You are book smart but emotionally stunted." So, we sat for 1½ hours sitting six feet apart, as the world isolation is still going on. We talked about the mistakes we had made, not necessarily about blame but more about our versions of the realities and what he wanted

44

going forward and what I wanted. I told him we could "date" and that I would not live with him again, not yet. I will not see him again till he sorts the mess he has created with this new Woman. He said that she is not me, and said, moving in and my health scare and me ignoring him totally for three weeks showed him that he cannot survive or live with anyone but me. I told him that is all any woman ever wants. I told him that our lives will have to change 100%. I shared that I am pondering a move to the sea, to live a simpler life and to move toward my goal of Life Coaching and to get a book published, and also that I do not expect him to just do what I want to get me back. He said he will do whatever he needs to do to make us work again as us is all he really wants. I told him that he needs to get some hobbies for himself. Learn to get out of his own head, help the local community and he needs to make our time together worthwhile, he said, "he will do whatever we need to make this work and live with more intention."

I asked him how serious he was and he said he was serious enough to cancel the divorce right now. So we shall see where this goes. If I am honest I am not going to tell anyone yet as it seems silly to give anyone false hope, including myself. We shall see if his actions match the intent. Firstly, he needs to let this poor woman down who he has suckered to move in, to try to fill his inner hole.

I heard from him again today and he told me that he had reached out to all the important people in my life including our kids to build bridges and to admit what a shit storm he has created. All these things shocked me but I was also pleasantly surprised. He also said that he had some counselling with our old counsellor to ask where the lines are from helping his 'girlfriend' and enabling her to stay attached as he is the only breadwinner now. I have told him that I will not/cannot be involved in that process as it's not my place, and he agreed I was right. He called me today to tell me that due to the Coronavirus his work has cut all low-level people and the Executives have taken a 20% pay cut, but he did not seem that stressed. He even admitted that he has put one of his Motorbikes up for sale, as maybe a way to help his girlfriend to move forward. Again, kindness and progress neither of which I had asked for.

We have been talking extensively these last few days, and I am feeling some red flags here. He says that now he will not tell me the timeline to their dating. He says that he will not tell me where or how they met, and he refuses to admit that they were not sleeping together when we slept together back around my birthday! So, I am piecing together my diary and it is just not adding up? I was gone for five days in Newquay and then the following week, I had a weird dream about Will and my dreams are normally premonitions. Then on New Year's Eve he said that he was in London seeing the Fireworks and staying in a hotel in London, which he would never do alone. I think he has lied about not being with her, yet the following weekend was the Weekend that I heard him talking to her on the phone in his bedroom and confronted him. Then he was getting ready to go to the US for six weeks, and you cannot tell me that in all that time they were not sleeping together, because within three weeks of him coming back from the US, they were moved in together! I am considering getting a private investigator. I do not believe it is over nor do I believe that the quick divorce thing was just a way to 'Move forward' through this. I think he has promised her a new life and marriage and I am not sure if he is having his cake and smearing the shit all over himself too!

I am angry that this is what I am still putting myself through. I will need to see this on his face to see if he is lying. For me it's not about her at all, it is 100% about the lying. He still cannot be trusted! When we spoke on the phone tonight it was all I could do not to tell him. He said, "Why do I feel like I have done something wrong and how will I be able to sleep tonight?" The pressure he puts on me for his happiness may be more than I can bear.

Today I was a participant in an online rave with my nephew in Newquay. We all got glittered, pigtailed and liquored up and danced like crazy 20-year-olds for four hours. It was so much fun! It got to about 10pm and I texted him and told him to come over; ugh bad alcohol driven choice! We talked, we bonded we kissed and he fell asleep in my arms. Whilst he was asleep he got a text and I knew deep down it was from the girlfriend. I told him to show me the text and he refused. So I told him to leave, but he got on his knees and said that she had just written, "So you are staying at your wife's overnight then?" Then she actually called! He ignored her call but told me that she rang because she probably wanted to know whether to lock up or not, and I told him it's 11.30pm and he was being naive, as was I. What am I doing here? Is this a big mistake? I wanted him so much, we kissed and I felt animalistic toward him and we had sex, then had mad regret about putting myself and her in that position. He then said he was going to go home which all seems strange to me, but what do I do, this is all so weird. Did I just make a huge mistake, lead him on, and sabotage all the progress I had made, give him false hope? Do I want this? He spins a web of lies and then gets so tangled there is no way out. Then he texts me four hours later and express's concern because he feels like I had the virus about 10 days ago. My reply was "I think my concerns are more valid than yours after what we just did!"

So, we continue to talk daily and meet to go for walks. We met at the old house and it suddenly dawns on me that the lease does not run out there for two more weeks. So he has been paying all the bills there and at their new place too. He said that she came with not a lot of furniture and that she is sleeping in Alyssa's old bed. Is that weird of him to let her do that, or is that just my neurosis?

I am lying in bed wondering if this is a wise choice. I am doing all the coaching, leading, and positive affirmations for/toward him and I am still not receiving anything. I need way more from this relationship. I want to feel wanted, needed, appreciated and desired and a huge part of me still feels like he is still seeing this girl. Apparently, he is going to pay the rent through the end of the year; red flag? He admitted today that he cancelled his last counselling session and that he sees taking antidepressants like a personality failing. He is also not sharing with anyone, not even his sisters, the true extent of how bad he has blown up his life. So, no mention of dating whilst we were together nor that he is still living with her! So many red flags for me still. Maybe a few days of not seeing each other is a good idea for me. He is pushing for a date for us to move down by the seaside and to put his stuff in my storage unit and to put his spare car near my house. He also plans to sell a motorcycle to bail the girlfriend out financially, it all sounds so sordid as I write this! Maybe I do need to reach out to her…

I just can't seem to get the need to actually see what she looks like? How he actually thought that a retail assistant could be his answer? It all just seems so very desperate. Am I just easier to go back to as opposed to him moving forward and how will he ever truly 'know himself' if he never actually lives alone?

We have talked maybe twice a day for the last week or so. We are expressing our concerns and actually talking things through. He admits that he gets stuck in the fight/flight cycle, I am the Fighter and he is the Flight, I think I am learning that trying to force him to confront his feelings/me is the 100% wrong thing to do within our relationship. So, we talk, express our feelings, worries, hopes and desires and we listen to the others perspective and actually really listen; it is refreshing and real. I think that we are both realising that life is all about uncertainty but if our foundation is strong then we can cohabit within our marriage and not lose ourselves.

I am not sure how this will progress but I am damn sure that I am struggling to give up on us after 20+ years. We shall wait and see how the process of getting his 'girlfriend' out of the rental place. He said he is advertising the place and seeing about getting someone to take over the lease. I on the other hand will eventually go back to work and then will let my Boss know that I am moving eventually.

I have to learn to fulfil my dreams and the Life Coaching is going well. If only I had more time and a bit more cash I could put that into advertising and really make this take off but I am aware that I am not allowed to have another paid position whilst I am furloughed.

In respect to him and me, so many red flags keep appearing.

He sent me a picture last night of a Margarita he had made for himself on the coffee table at his house, surrounded by girly accessories that were not ours. He tells me that they do not talk and barely communicate yet he said that she dropped him off at the old house so he could drive his motorcycle back to their house. My gut tells me to hire that Private Investigator and see what details they can get. I also understand that the fact he is already cohabiting even before we are divorced is a huge no-no! They are going to get some photos of them together and get me her contact details. I need to know what he promised her to make her move herself and her 10-year-old kid in with him. Can I do this? Should I? A big part of me does not feel like this can ever work after the indifference, lies, infidelity, and lack of responsibility. I think way too much murky and dirty water has gone under the bridge! Plus, better to know than not know

Just received the move out summary from the house we shared together via email and within that is his current address, scanning through it and my phone rings and it is my sister. I tell her that I want to drive over there, and I asked her if I was being crazy. My Sister asked to see a picture of the girlfriend as she was interested in what I was replaced with and so I sent her the picture. She was shocked that she was Asian, and then she said something that changed everything! "Do you remember the bank charges that he had racked thousands of dollars up at a Massage Parlour that were in the Bank Records that the Lawyers have for the financial disclosure, could that be where he met her?" I just felt all the pieces fit together in my head!

How in the hell did I ever think that I could make this work! What am I thinking, he will not ever change and nor do

I want or need him to. He is a disgusting man! I texted him after a sleepless night and asked him to meet me, his reply, "OK".

I drove there feeling sick and shaking I got there a few minutes before him and tried to breathe…

He pulled up, got out of his car and walked toward me. He smiled at me and I looked away and I suggested we find somewhere to sit. He followed me over to some benches at the other side of the carpark and we sat. He asked what was wrong, I said, "I am about to ask you something, and I already know the answer so please do not lie, and when I say it, it will change everything." He looked petrified, so I took a deep breath and said "What town did you meet your girlfriend and where did she work?" He paused, I exhaled and he said "Windsor." I felt such a surge of emotion, I got up and I said, "She worked at that Massage Parlour you spent a fortune at didn't she?"

He looked shocked and replied, "Yes," and I told him that he was a cliché male Mid-Life Crisis. I was so upset and he asked why it made a difference where she worked. I did try to explain my emotion but he did not understand why where she works makes any difference to me. He had stated previously that he wanted to build our new foundation on honesty and I told him that our new foundation was built on a lie. I asked if it was even true that they no longer spoke or texted each other and he said that he did not message her anymore and that he had even blocked her on a couple of platforms. I asked if that was the case then show me your phone, he grabbed his phone, put it in his lap to try to delete stuff and I told him not to bother. If the tables were turned I would have just handed over my phone as I have nothing to hide; shame that he cannot say

51

the same! I told him that I deserve so much better than this, and that I could never trust him nor feel like I could ever have sex with him again. He cried on and off throughout our interaction and could not look me in the eye, maybe embarrassed or maybe annoyed at getting caught in the web of lies he has spun! He asked me if I would consider how he can change and try to make this work between us as he only wants to be with me. I told him that he does not want to truly be with me and that he needs to be by himself. I reiterated that I now have zero trust in him nor could I sleep with him and that maybe I am not willing to make any compromise for him now. He asked me to text him later to talk and I said not today I won't.

Woke up today to the message that said "He understands that there is no way to build back what is broken. He remembered that I told him that he was a middle-aged cliché and that I stated that I am better than this. He said that all of these things we cannot possibly move forward with our relationship" If I am 100% honest with myself, this was all just a means to a messy end really. I shall now block him, wallow for a few days/weeks again and push forward with my original plan to move on with my life because in reality, what choice do I have…but before that I need to write a letter to the girlfriend in my best "Crazy ex-wife rant" and drive it over to their house and put in on her car windscreen. I warned her of his narcissistic personality and his cycle of control, I told her that he will promise her and her son the World; that he will promise her Marriage and security but the price for that would be that he would be on a Marriage visa instead of a work visa. I told her he will control everything they do and will cry and pout till he gets his way. I let her know that he was sleeping with her and me back in November and that he has been actively pursuing me the last month. I wrote that I hold no ill will toward her and understood how charming he can be and to be careful. I wrote my number in the letter so she could call/text to verify anything she wanted, and I take it from his frantic "OMG" texts I received three hours later that he had in fact read the letter. A Woman scorned!

How dare he think that he can have his cake and eat it too? It is obvious from his reaction that she is not just a roommate at all.

Another sleepless night and another letter written, so I get dressed and drive over there and when I get to the door I am not sure what to do so I just knock on the door and no answer so then I just knock on the living room window. He comes to the door and I tell him that I want to talk to her. He tells me 'NO' and says that we can walk and talk, I tell him again I want to talk to her; he said let's walk through gritted teeth! So I walk and he tells me that he is the victim in this and that I have literally broken his life. He threatens me with going back to the US and I tell him that he should. He said, he has already talked to his sister and I shrug my shoulders. He asks me if I have ever cheated and I told him that I have not, so we talk and he continues to tell me that he is not broken, to which I reply, "Yes I know that?" He says that he is never good enough and that he is not an 'unfillable cup,' he said that he is not a Narcissist and that's just my buzzword. I just replied, "Alright". He said that I did not know his mom and dad as well as I had thought and they did not love me. I replied, "You are talking out of anger and spite and I did know and love your Parents like they were my own. I then look him in the eye and ask him if he is 100% done with us and he replies, "Yes!" well thank goodness. He walks back toward his house and I decide to sit in my car and wait to talk to her. Five minutes later he drives by, pulls over to my car, gets out and says "Are you just going to sit here and harass me?" I told him again that I came here to talk to her. He gets in his car and drives off.

Fifteen minutes go by and she pulls back into the road and I wave her down. She drives past me and reverses back onto the pavement, she gets out of her car and walks toward me and we both start crying and she comes to hug me! All I want to do is sob, but she says, let's go back to the house and have a cup of tea and I agreed. I leave my car and she invites me into her car and we drive back to her house, when she pulls onto the driveway he looks through the curtains and comes to the door and says "You are not coming in this house!" she told him, "This is my house too and I invited her here." She gently pushes by him and he followed us into the kitchen. He said "You are destroying my life, what are you doing here?" She told him to go away and work and he just stood there. She pushed his hand off the door frame and the fridge and gently pushed him out of the door and closed it behind him, he was shouting something and all I heard was the front door slamming! She looked at me and said that she was so sorry. I said the same thing I expressed regret that she had not reached out to me after the letter I wrote and she informed me that she never received a letter. She mentioned that she had wanted to reach out to me on Facebook but she had blocked him on there so that friendship suggestion never popped up again. I told her that I am sorry that he had put her in this position and she proceeded to tell me that she was shy and needed a glass of wine and asked if I minded. She invited me into the living room, large glass of wine in hand; it was really unnerving to see all the things I had collected over the last 25 years strewn around this house that was not mine. She then proceeded to tell me about her wonderful daughter and her handsome son who is 9, she showed me pictures, days out, her friends, videos of the family home her father had built in Thailand about her large family, she then facetimed with her best friend in Australia and the three of us talked about life, relationships and how wonderful it is that we could finally talk to each other, She said that her ex-husband looks after their son because the living situation is so weird at the house and that she has always slept with her son. The Marriage with his dad did not work out as he is 17 years her senior but he is a great dad. The son does not feel a connection to this new house or his Mum's boyfriend; he is a distraction from his relationship with his Mum so he chooses to stay at his dad's house instead. She shared that she has recently sold a plot of land in Thailand to help finance her 20-year-old daughter. She then said that her Great Aunt is going to start paying her 1k a month to help her get back on her feet again after the lockdown is finished. She talked about the strange conversation she had with him about the kids and money. In this conversation he had said that he knew their relationship could never work. She shared that he had flushed his wedding ring down the toilet to prove how serious he was about them. Funny how there are always two parts to a story! She told me that she had only been in the UK for 10 years and that she was taking written/spoken English classes online as she struggles with both. I told her that I am still relearning Pounds/Ounces/Fahrenheit after living in the US for 16 years and told her that after another 3-5 years it will all become automatic and that your English is great. She requested a bathroom break, after she called me upstairs to show me the bedroom situation and whose bathroom is whose and the room that she works out in. She seems so mature for her age with an inner strength, not what I was expecting but it drew me to her. I could actually be Friends with this person.

She runs and works out too. She tells me that she was told I live in Wokingham, so I corrected that, and her ex lives literally right up the street from me, small world! I told her that I am done with him and that I wish her the very best and to concentrate on the lessons we are both learning. I apologised in advance for the crying wreck he would be when he returned and she said that she was immune to his crying too. I walked back to my car and sat there for a while and actually felt like I could breathe again; this has to be over. I cannot live in this headspace anymore, it is emotionally exhausting! I cried a lot on and off today and am sleep deprived and adrenaline driven right now, and hope this ends soon.

Late afternoon on the same day I receive an email from my solicitor stating that his withdrawal of the divorce may not have gone through so maybe still valid. If the withdrawal has been processed, he will have to start from scratch again and that he is withdrawing all financial agreements between us. His email said that he will now wait for my divorce filing on the grounds of adultery and will proceed accordingly. He added that he burned all the pictures of me that he has too! I knew it would get hateful and apparently here it is. I am actually thinking I am not going to do anything at all divorce wise. He has not given me a penny in the last five months so another 12 months won't make much of a difference. Maybe I just need to continue to move forward with the knowledge that what I have in the bank is it and make my peace with it—throughout the night I received 22 emails telling me how he was the complete victim in our whole relationship. He stated that a platonic relationship we both had with a couple that lived and worked with us in South Dakota was the seed that slowly festered and slowly killed our marriage. Strange as I have not had any physical sexual contact with any man aside from him in 25 years! Well I suppose our realities are different when jaded by pain and hurt and I understand that. I should at some point write to apologise that I did not trust him on the fact that he was really finished with the girlfriend but it was all such a weird situation of texts and phone calls and defending her profession toward the end. To be honest, he lies by omission so much that it is always difficult to find the middle ground or truth.

He suggested that I will not be keeping half of 'His inheritance' and I am pondering whether to share it with the kids so as it is no longer an issue…I shall ponder.

The girlfriend invited me over to their house at 6pm and she said she was lonely and sad there, and needed the company so I went and she had apparently told him three hours prior that I was coming and sent him to the shops to buy food and snacks I would like. I sat and he floated in and out of the living room bringing in snacks and being social, nice yet unusual to see! So we sat and we talked about our day and our kids and their plans, her long term plans to go back to Thailand and he said, "Oh I did not know any of that," I asked him if he had read my earlier email about how men and women communicate differently and how only knowing ¼ of the truth leads to the madness we make up in our own heads! He said he had read it and saw the correlation.

She and I drank wine and cider and he had a rum and coke but he did not drink till 11pm. We talked and talked and he ends up just going off to bed without saying a word at around 1am. The two of us talked, she held my hand for another hour or so and then she went up to bed. I decided to go up and sleep fully clothed in his room as I was drunk. I get into his bed and he reaches over and touches my arm, he reaches down to touch me and then gets up and goes to the bathroom so I take off my jeans. When he came back and kissed me and I heard him say "I love you" all of a sudden he gets up saying "I can't do this!" and starts retching like he needs to be sick! I get up and get dressed and go downstairs and he is crouched in the corner of the living room retching!! He goes upstairs into her bedroom and is crying so I just sit there in the living room contemplating what to do; I am too drunk to drive. After about 15 minutes she comes downstairs and tells me that he said that he had thought it was her coming into his bed! In which case why would he do what he did and why would he say that he loves her? She told him "When have I ever sneaked into your bed?" We had a cup of tea and I told her to go to bed as it is 3.30am at this point. I decided to just go sleep in his bed and stay dressed and when I try he gets up and says that he cannot do this anymore, so I get up and put on my shoes and drive home! What an absolute drama fuelled nightmare. Why in the hell do I keep doing this to myself!

When I woke up I pondered what an absolute nightmare the last week had been, my phone showed that both him and her had called and texted to see if I got home alright, I am shocked that I drove like that, I have NEVER done that and never would again. I recall how lucky I was that at 3.45am and that there was not another single car on the road! And how I absolutely should have stayed put till I had slept!

Her and I texted a lot the next two days and she shared how she knew that within a few days that it would have not worked with him; there was too much crying, her child did not connect with him and an incident where he flushed our wedding ring had changed her view on him.

Meanwhile, he and I are still texting back and forth and trying to be better about how we communicate and talk things through and also trying to laugh and be friends again.

I invited him over three days later and we had a couple of drinks in my tiny room and talked and talked, he held me tight and breathed me in, I reached out to him and kissed him and he was hesitant but I soon persuaded him and we made love like we had many years before with deep emotion and feeling. It was so great, sadly if there is alcohol involved, he cannot finish but I reminded myself NOT to take on the blame for that and just reminded him it is all about the connection for me and that topic just faded away. This is craziness! What the hell am I doing, it's a cycle of my own madness!!

We got up early and went over to his place, he said that there is something he needs to share, I gulped and reminded myself to listen and regulate my reaction, understanding him instead of high emotion. He said "I need you to know firstly that I burned every picture of you and I flushed our wedding ring and I gave her 8k so she can restart her life." I did not tell him that she had told me all of that aside from the money. I told him I understood and in the scheme of things none of that stuff is important. I tried to remind him, and his guilt, that she is indeed a strong woman and she played a part in the demise of this too. When we got back to his place it seems like she had packed a few bags and left for a while.

We sat silently for a while and I told him I appreciated his honesty and we decided to go for a run. During the run he stopped to wait for me at corners, he let me know if cars were coming around a blind spot, caring things he used to do when we were deeply connected and I really appreciated that. When we came back we showered and went food shopping. I made lunch for us both and we just sat looking at each other holding hands which soon ended up as us in bed deep connecting again.

We spent the rest of the day talking about places we wanted to go to rewrite the trips we had taken, it seemed then we were so disconnected that I am not sure how we survived!

He talked about where he wanted to go within his job, how he wanted to do consultancy work and write, and how we should think about living together again and maybe waiting to move again till March 1st when the lease ends. I said that I wanted to concentrate on writing too and that I wanted my Coaching to progress and that I wanted to talk to my boss about not working all day Saturdays anymore. We talked about weekends away, cycling in the countryside and just being together. I have noticed that his phone is turned off. I told him that I did not expect him to always have it off and that he still has unfinished business with the girlfriend and as long as it is 100% over for him, then I am not going to get stressed if she texts him. He said that he wanted to learn to be more in the moment and he is turning off his work phone too; I appreciated his honesty. It has been a really lovely couple of days after an emotional rollercoaster this last month. We see each other and understand that we both need alone time too and there is no guilt or ill will when we separate for a while; it is actually the best of both worlds.

After the 'girlfriend' had been gone a few days I decided I was, with her permission via text message, now comfortable spending time over at his house. So I went over in the evening and we decided we would run first thing in the morning so I took my gear for running and a change of clothes and shower products. The following morning, after the run we both showered and decided to go out for a motorcycle ride. It was a beautiful warm day and so we toured around for a couple of hours and then returned back to the house.

It appears that whilst we were out she had been to the house and taken her coffee maker and iPod dock. I asked him if she had texted him, he went to get his phone and the onslaught started, "You are both awful people, why did you move all of my stuff. I am going to file a report as I have rights in that house too, can't you both wait till I completely move out!" I saw the wave of panic within him building. I asked him if he still had feelings for her and if he was having doubts. He turned that around and put it on me by asking if I was having doubts about moving in to which I replied "I am not having doubts I just will not be anyone's second choice!"

The onslaught continued and she stated that she was coming back with her son to sleep for a few days and that she did not know what to do now. His panic was mounting to frenzy and so I told him that I was going to remove myself from the situation so he could deal with this. Strangely he did not argue the fact, nor did he tell her it is over and to move on, he just kept saying that he did not understand 'her crazy'. I told him that this only coming from one of two places, Wanting the relationship to work again or wanting more sympathy and in turn more money. I think that now we have shared all that she has told us both, the puzzle pieces have started to "Fit" more clearly but again people's lives and their paths are exactly that. Let's just say that she has made, in my estimation/judgement quite a few questionable decisions. Arranged marriage at 18, daughter born and then divorced, new boyfriend she met in a different Country 17 years her senior, left her daughter in another Country to marry here and had a son, divorced straight away, son now living with his dad. Her Parents do not know what she does for a living nor that she is divorced. Need I say more?

I get back to my place and feel relieved that I did not tell my Landlord I was moving. I needed some alone time after two days there, I am not sure if this is a good thing right now or not?

I feel like if this was me, I would tell myself that "I had paid for her life for the last 3+ months, I gave her 8K to pay her rent going forward, I am paying for the movers at her request, and I am sure there is other stuff I do not know either! Maybe this is not over for him whether it is guilt, regret or wanting a second chance to try to figure this out!! He calls me this morning and express's remorse at me having to leave, he admits that he told her he cared about her to try to get her over here and I told him it is all very strange that she has not reached out to me but reinforced to him that she will, I guarantee it! I told him to try to pick a path and be happy with the decision, he apologised for trying to manipulate her to try her to come over and I suggested that if she texts him today he tell her to come over then ignore her texts till she does, he agreed then a moments silence, I asked if he had got a text and he said he had not but then stated he was not feeling well and that he was going to go lay down, I did not hang up the call and could hear him texting, I think he is caught up in the lie, drama of all of this and I am just going to leave him to this till it is done.

He came over to mine yesterday and we went for a walk, whilst we were walking I told him that I would not be moving in Saturday as we had previously talked about, he asked why and if I was not sure of "Us" again and told him that I was but that four days prior I had to leave that house because he was texting his ex-girlfriend and it all seemed too soon and that I was enjoying the dating thing, he accepted that. I asked him also what women want from relationships to see if he was learning, he said communication and time and I added passion, we need passion, Once we were done walking we came back here and had lunch and after 20 minutes TV watching he had to go because he had work calls to do, I told him I was going to spend the afternoon pleasuring myself, hoping to spark something in him to stay but no, that was a bust!

He called me the next morning and I asked if the "Ex" had showed up yesterday as planned and he said that she did not and that she had texted him to say that she was not feeling well nor sleeping so was skipping coming over to pack, apparently the movers are still coming on Friday to move her stuff out, he did say that he had contacted the rental agency to advise them to take her off the lease as authorised tenants, I suppose that is progress.

Part of me still feels like things will not change enough for me within our relationship, I need more passion than he can muster, I want a man that considers me, I want someone who is handy, that is so strange but has become such a "thing" for me, I feel like I have become the "male persona" within our relationship and that he takes on such an emotional role that I just cannot be my real emotional self as that much oestrogen within one relationship is just too much!

Can we make this work or has too much crying and bad feeling made this impossible to move forward? Why am I so scared to just call it!?

We continue to walk and talk, shop and ponder our future together, I continue to press for real conversations and feel a pathetic need to be comforted and reassured that he wants "Us" I feel torn as to whether to fully engage, to move in, to add myself to the tenancy and bills, when I get emails from him, I anticipate that he is again telling me that we could never work out. I suppose trust will take some time to rebuild so I shall continue to read, learn, progress with my own stuff outside of our relationship and maybe keep my place for a couple months to be sure.

The sex thing seems to be an issue, or maybe it is a "me thing", I feel as sexually attracted to him as I have ever felt and because he is on antidepressants his sex drive is not even at zero! I am not immature enough to say silly stuff like "Aren't you attracted to me anymore!" but it has affected my confidence a little, he still drinks too much and eats garbage but that is his issue not mine, I am not his mother but we are having productive calm conversations, working through issues and stressors that come up, going out running, motorcycling, all I am missing is sex, but in reality he is in his 50s so that may well be a thing of the past, but it will be a subject I have to brooch and so I did, he said that his antidepressants do affect his sex drive but he said that the Viagra corrects that in an hour and helps his ego to continue to feel like an 18 year old whilst having sex. He continued to tell me that it is not about his passion for me and I informed him that I am not so immature to be mired in sadness that he does not find me attractive anymore, I feel as attractive and as sexual as I have ever felt and that I can sort myself out if need be. He did joke that I am the masculine more highly sexed one in our relationship now so I told him to get upstairs, have a shower and get in bed and wait for me, when I got upstairs he was lying in a quintessentially female pose, we both laughed then I ravaged him, afterwards I told him to go make me a sandwich and again we giggled.

I do think and feel like our relationship is more grown up and calm although I do have to still be cautious as we are only a week in. He is still a reactionary being who is addicted to shopping online, we food shop nearly every other day, we have a whole freezer full and a large and a small fridge too! I have to remind myself that there is no such thing as a perfect relationship nor a perfect person and that everyone we cohabit with has their own quirks.

Learning that he is driven by the need for companionship and touch has been relatively easy to correct for me and I am proud of what we have accomplished in the last few weeks. We have had a great couple of weeks here and I have been back to my place a few times. I do actually wonder how I would live there long term as the owners that live there 6 months out of the year, are the untidiest people, the kitchen is constantly in a state of disarray, it is almost like she is constantly filling time, in a strange twist though, she does beautiful flowers arrangements and they are all around. I know I am probably rationalising this, but I am not sure if we were not working on our own relationship that I could live there long term, how and when would I be able to cook as she never leaves the kitchen! Plus I know I am a neat freak but again that is a "Me" issue.

So, it looks like the Universe has forced my hand here. For me to be legally able to move back in with him, I need to get a reference from my current Landlord so I had to tell them via email that I am moving out in the next few weeks.

So, onto the next chapter...